DeAR L█████

WWBD?

Dear DANA,

.WWBD?

[signature]

Written by Scott Carbonara
Cover design by Chris Popieluszko

© 2010
Fourth Printing December 2010

Table of Contents

Synopsis

Have you ever felt like it is too late to start over? Told through a story of how an unwanted dog became a life-changing mentor, *Firsthand Lessons, Secondhand Dogs* is a book about getting a second chance at enjoying a first-rate existence. The story begins with the unlikely adoption of a "secondhand" dog, Bruno, and is paralleled to the life of his "adoptive father," author Scott Carbonara. As Scott's life changes, through work promotions and challenges, Bruno subtly yet strongly demonstrates how to have fun, focus, forgive, and finally, pay it forward--all lessons that serve us whether in business or life. As Scott illustrates through poignant, often humorous stories and accompanying lessons and exercises, as long as you strive to keep learning and teaching others, your work continues. This book provides an opportunity to laugh, learn, and love your life again, all while finding concrete ways to pay it forward.

Praise for *Firsthand Lessons, Secondhand Dogs*

Scott's gifted story-telling underlies humble and applicable lessons. As I read, I was laughing, crying, and thinking about how I could become a better person and manager. We are all apt to find ourselves in the position of being a "secondhand dog" at some point in our lives. Scott's book provides the upside to reinvention.

- Jocelyn Godfrey, President, Spiritus Communications, Inc.

Funny, warm, insightful...*Secondhand Dogs* reminds us that "as long as we have the capability to learn, our work improving our world is never complete." Through small and seemingly simple events, the lessons learned from these two secondhand dogs are HUGE, and they can be applied to anyone from student, teacher, mentor, friend, parent. Prepare for this book to make a huge impact on your thinking and in your life.

- Gina Gagliano, Veteran Educator and New Teacher Mentor/Coordinator

Firsthand Lessons is perfect for anyone wanting to excel in life or leadership and is a great example that no matter what your role in life, it's never too late to reinvent and create a life of excellence.

- Marlene Chism, Author of Stop Workplace Drama

This book impacted me with its simple wisdom. Normally, I read a few pages of a book, and if I haven't gotten the message yet, I know I never will. The relationship between Scott and Bruno, however, engaged me to turn pages, see what would happen next, and finish the whole book! I learned a lot about myself in the process, as I reflected on moments of my life. The message and lessons are relative to the times, but also timeless. I energetically put *Firsthand Lessons, Secondhand Dogs*, on anyone's "must-read-now" list.

- Sam Glenn, Speaker, Author of A Kick in the Attitude, *and founder of EverythingAttitude.com*

BRUNO	ME	YOU	ACTIONS

A quick explanation about the icons above is in order:

The 1st icon represents Bruno. He is the original secondhand dog. When you see that icon, you know that there is a story or two about Bruno coming.

The 2nd icon symbolizes me, the other secondhand dog. These are the sections where I applied the wisdom Bruno taught me in the corporate world.

11

The 3rd icon stands for you, the reader. These segments are designed to help you think through the lessons and figure out how you can apply them in your own life.

The 4th icon is a place to challenge your thinking and compel you into action. Don't cheat yourself on the application portion. Insight without application will take you only so far.

Bruno meets Bruno.

Note from a Secondhand Dog:

Have you ever felt broken down, or second-rate? I have. That's why I wrote this book. I want to share some simple secrets that I learned years ago from my best friend.

I had this dog who came into my life during a critical period of my young adulthood. I was living in a new place far from my family and friends. The only person I knew was my wife. I was working in a new job, one that required snap judgment regarding life and death matters. I was overloaded with work and graduate school, and I crammed and wrote papers when I should have been sleeping. In a very real way, I had no time for friends. Except one very special dog who became my best friend.

This dog was self-taught. He had no college degree. I never saw him write things down, or read a book. I never even saw him looking at pictures in magazines or glancing at the comics. He was taken away from his mother when he was too young to remember her face; the family who took him in abandoned him with a stranger once his cuteness wore off. The world had not been kind to my little friend, but my friend refused to view himself as tragically flawed. He refused to view himself as a victim. He returned unkindness with kindness; and he learned to trust and love again. Self-taught, yes, but he was an amazing teacher.

Since that day I got him more than twenty years ago, my life has changed many times over. I've moved several more times and worked many different jobs, some of them in completely new fields. I moved from subject-matter expert into management, proficient doer into learning-as-I-go leader. I've become a father, twice. I've experienced losses. And I've had many more pets.

While I have felt broken down by life, and I have felt like a second-rate person more than once in those twenty years, this isn't a book about being defeated. This is a story of renewal and victory. These are lessons that I applied to help me become a better, happier person.

Refuse to view yourself or your experiences as second class. As long as you strive to keep learning and teaching others, your work continues. It's never too late for a secondhand dog to enjoy a first-rate life. Once you get it, make sure you share what you learned with others.

Now it's time for me to pay it forward. I hope you enjoy my story.

🐾 Scott Carbonara

Epilogue

I know, I know. It's customary to begin a book with a prologue and to end a book with an epilogue. But sometimes it's better to know how it all ends, so here goes: Bruno is happy and I have moved on.

For Bruno, it was easy. He didn't waste a single moment lost in reflection or second-guessing his every action. He just lived. He knew how to enjoy himself, and how to bring joy to others. He knew how to bring joy to me. In a way, I am his creation. Somewhere along the way when I stopped to watch him eat the roses, I was changed. And in a very real sense, he makes a leap onto the edge of my bed and into my heart each day. For him, his second chance was his first opportunity to really live.

Although I took a different path, the destination ended up at the same place. Admittedly, I wasted much time reliving every moment, wondering what-if-I-had-only-done-this-instead-of-that? In a funny way, Bruno would have admired my ability to spend six months reviewing the tapes of my life before coming to the same conclusion a friend of mine told me on the day my life was changed again:

I believe there is something much bigger and more beautiful than you can imagine waiting out there for you.

Not every day is full of sunshine. Not every cookie has extra chocolate chips. Not every songbird sits outside your window to sing for you--sometimes that bird just swoops down to streak crap across your windshield. Friendships will come into your life, and they will go. People will please you; others will disappoint you. You will have jobs you love as well as ones you hate.

The key is to keep going after a setback, to keep pushing forward. There is new life in second chances.

I'm moving on, Bruno. It's time for me to let go of some things that could slow me down as I take my next step into the unknown. I'm proud of what I have accomplished so far, but I'm uncertain about what the morrow brings. I'm keeping my head held high; what better way to see the new day coming?

While I leave some things behind, I'm keeping what you taught me close to my heart. Thanks, little guy.

Introduction: Your Life is Going to Change

As my twenty-fifth birthday approached, my wife gave me two options for a present. I could get a dog, or I could get something else that I won't even pretend to remember. It might have been new skis or a yacht. It didn't matter; I wanted the dog!

My family briefly had a dog when I was a child. I say briefly because the thing kept running away. He spent most of his time "on the lam." Fluffy was a high-strung, mean-spirited, yappy miniature Poodle. When I was five, my dad filmed me chasing Fluffy. I would go to one corner of the shed and peak around. Sensing me, Fluffy would bolt around the corner and disappear. I would run to where Fluffy had just been, and once again he'd go POOF just as I arrived. To the untrained eye, it looked like we were playing. It was not play. The dog had escaped his leash again, and I was trying to retrieve him. I think my dad filmed the whole scene in case he was ever brought up on criminal charges for screaming the dog to death. He figured no jury would convict him if he had film evidence proving how rotten and disobedient the dog could be.

Having Fluffy was like trying to own smoke or cuddle with the wind. I didn't like Fluffy. He was a self-centered, spastic, Q-tip topped dog, incapable of loving or being loved. Eventually, my parents gave him to a relative in the country so the dog could run without ever being considered "away."

No, I didn't like Fluffy. But I loved dogs, at least the concept of dogs, dogs that would play, come, fetch, roll over, sit, and not run away. I had never had one, but I was convinced that it would be a great experience for me. Along with things like jumping on the bed, drinking milk out of the jug, and turning the thermostat above sixty-two degrees in the wintertime, I added DOG OWNER to the list of things I would do or be when I no longer lived with my parents.

Fast forward twenty years. I was driving in a little town in northern Wisconsin when just before a gravel road I saw a sign posted that announced:

"Yorkshire Terrier Puppy's 4 Sale."

I didn't know what a Yorkshire Terrier was, but the sign included a painting that approximated a dog in that it had hair, pointy ears, and a black nose. Thinking back, it may have been a painting of a bear. That's not important. What is important is that my wife said, "I know you've always wanted a dog, Honey. But you know it makes absolutely no sense for us to get an animal at this stage of our lives. But since your birthday is coming…"

"*YES!*" I screamed as I pulled down the gravel road. I'm sure she was about to say that I could have a dog even though it didn't make sense right now. But I wasn't willing to hear her finish for fear it would end with "…you can have anything EXCEPT a dog."

I couldn't have known at the time that this event would mark a series of defining moments for me. What I wanted was a little, friendly dog. What I got was a large lesson in how to live.

A new start for an old cast-away.

The breeder was a middle-aged woman who claimed nearly twenty years experience breeding Yorkshire Terriers. Currently, she had a litter of four puppies. These were young puppies, just opening their eyes. They each weighed about eight ounces, and could fit on my flat palm with plenty of room to spare. They were all black, and their ears flopped over. The breeder explained that their ears wouldn't stand up for another couple of weeks. I loved them all.

How could something be that tiny?!

I was a little overwhelmed and very excited. If I'd had a tail, it would have been wagging hard. How could I choose which one of these little guys to take home?

From the next room, I heard a growl and some barking. The breeder said, "Toby! Quiet!"

I asked her if Toby was the father of the pups.

"No," she said sadly. "Toby's owner asked me to take him in. Toby's parents were AKC champion dogs, so the lady who bought him paid a lot of money for him. Spent $800. But when the novelty of having a little dog wore off, she neglected him. He's spent most of his three years of life in a dog crate, poor little guy. His back is hunched up from being cramped, and he's too small to consider using him as a breeder. Defective genes."

How ugly can he be? I wondered. I asked if I could see him.

When she opened the cage, Toby stood halfway out of the doorway for a moment, his body still. He had long, matted hair. He looked like a picture I had seen once of the Wild Men of Borneo twins. As Toby came completely out of the crate, I flashed back to Fluffy. Toby's eyes locked onto me, and he managed a few guttural growls. He straightened up his full four-pound frame as best he could, and then charged me with a full yap.

I hated him instantly.

I jumped back and gave a little nervous laugh. "He's pretty spunky," I observed. I thought but didn't say aloud, *I hate spunky.*

"He hasn't been socialized. My puppies are held and played with all of the time. That's how you socialize puppies. But if you don't do it when they are real young, they don't warm up to people."

By now, Toby had quieted down and was standing a few feet away, looking at me intently. I squatted down, and Toby thanked me by backing up, barking, and then launching towards me again with hard, mean eyes. I held my ground. *Little turd*, I thought. *I'm not intimidated by you.* It didn't take long before Toby quieted down again and seemed to relax a little. Slowly, he started to come towards me. I held out the back of my hand. The barking fired up again, but this time it stopped more quickly. Soon, Toby was sniffing my hand. I stroked his little, hunched frame with the back of my hand. He growled but didn't move.

Within a few minutes, I was sitting crossed-legged on the floor, and Toby was leaning into me so I could pet him.

"So what are you going to do with him if you can't breed him? Is he your pet?" I asked the breeder.

"Oh, no," she responded quickly. "I don't deal in secondhand dogs. Toby's just here until I get the time to have him put down."

Five minutes later, Toby was crated in the backseat of our car as we headed home.

Change makes us vulnerable.

Toby stayed in his cage while the "adults" talked up front.

"The name has to go," my wife said.

"Absolutely," I agreed.

We drove the two hours home discussing names. Nothing seemed to fit. We both liked the idea of an ironic name. *Killer* came to mind because he was so little, but having heard him bark and growl, *Killer* was less ironic than an accurate warning to others. *Butch* and *Brutus* were overused. We were still tossing out names as we approached our home in Crystal Falls, Michigan, and drove past the gas station on the edge of town.

Bruno's was one of only three pumps in town, and in addition to selling gasoline, Bruno's had one more claim to fame that was something I had never before seen: an honest automobile mechanic! Bruno's son, Keane, was a genius with cars. Since I drove an old car, I was no stranger to repair shops. The high-tech equipment in Chicago could not come close to the expertise that Bruno and Keane had in diagnosing and repairing. And they didn't say stuff like, "Ahh, your Bloiken rod that sticks through the Tie shaft has to be deburred or it will strip your co-axle converter belt right down to the nib. You're looking at about $1,200." No, Bruno and Keane would fix the problem, spare me the lies, and charge me a low price.

My wife and I exchanged looks and said at the same moment, "Bruno!"

There was a bark of agreement from the backseat. It was settled. We had a name that was not only ironic but also an oxymoron since the real Bruno was a one-of-a-kind, honest mechanic.

Once home, things became chaotic. First up, Bruno's mangy, knotted hair had to go. *No problem*, I thought. *I have clippers.*

I quickly came to understand that Bruno wasn't a fan of sudden, metallic noises like hair trimmers starting up near his body. When I first turned them on, Bruno whipped around and sank his mouthful of needles into the back of my hand. Two hours later, Bruno's hair was gashed and hacked like he had lost a knife fight, and my hands and arms were bleeding from where he had scratched and bitten me.

Bath time followed. I was to find out that Bruno was actually more tolerant of the idea of dying by hair clippers than he was of drowning. As soon as I hoisted him over the water, some primitive survival instinct set in, and Bruno's legs kicked into Four-Wheel-Scratch. When he was wet, he looked like an ugly, hunch-backed rat, only less cute. He added new bites and scratches to my body. *How are you supposed to wash something that has sharp, pointy things on every end?* I wondered.

Next up was training. Bruno had never worn a collar or leash. *How hard can it be to teach him?* I thought. Turns out, it was pretty hard. Bruno responded to my tugging on the leash by lying flat on the ground and digging in with all twenty nails. After fifteen minutes of dragging him around the yard, we were both ready to call it a day. When I knelt down to unhook his leash, he bit me.

My attempts to change Bruno into a less smelly, better groomed, and more disciplined dog had cost me three deep bites and about thirty scratches.

We were all pooped. I made up a little sleeping area for Bruno inside his crate, figuring he might be more comfortable in a familiar place. He ran inside immediately and lay down on the blanket. I collapsed on the bed while my wife showered.

A few moments later, I felt a quick vibration on my bed. Looking up, I saw Bruno had jumped on the edge of the mattress and was looking at me with his head cocked slightly and his ears standing straight up. I reached over to my nightstand and grabbed this finger puppet that had been a free giveaway from the Little Caesars pizza shop as a promotion. I slipped my finger inside the puppet and said, "Pizza, pizza!" Bruno launched himself at my finger. He attacked, pulling the puppet free from my grasp, and shook it in his mouth so quickly it made a whipping sound in the air. Then he dropped it in front of me. I put Little Caesar back on, and the game continued. And continued. And continued.

Bruno wasn't a natural when it came to meeting strangers. He wasn't fond of haircuts. He was decidedly displeased with baths. And I think we were both dreading going outside for his morning drag around the yard. But Bruno was gifted when it was time to play.

My memories about the earlier struggles of the day, the ones when Bruno did everything in his power to hurt me before I could have a chance to hurt him, were fading. Playing with him there on my bed, I saw a different animal than the one who had been so casually cast away when his cuteness and newness had worn off. I wasn't seeing a snippy, yappy, mean-spirited dog with a hunched back and bad genes. I was seeing a passionate, playful puppy of three living for the first time in his life.

I decided at that moment that I loved him.

When my wife came out of the shower, Bruno was lying down next to me with his head resting on Little Caesar. And I was wiping my eyes.

"What's wrong? Is he hurt?" She asked.

"No," I said sniffling. "He's perfect, and I love him."

She gave me a look that showed she understood what I meant.

I don't know if she could have understood what was behind my tears. I didn't understand it myself. My day had started like every other day. Then the birthday offer. The thought of a puppy. The roller coaster at the breeder when my heart cried out for this mean, humped up little four-pound bruiser. Picking a name made him mine and real. Me cutting his hair and him cutting my hands and arms made me feel like I had earned his love. The playing we had just done cemented the bond even further.

I was crying because if I could love this little dog so quickly and deeply after such an unexpected, challenging start, what would I do if I ever lost him?

Opening myself up to loving Bruno made me vulnerable. Emotional vulnerability is essential for growth. I had a lot of growth in front of me.

Weighty Lessons from a Four-Pound Dog

Bruno came into my life at a time when I was defining who I was as a person. I was living in a new place far from my family and friends. The only person I knew was my wife. I was working a new job, one that required snap judgment over matters that could bring life or death. I was overloaded with work and graduate school, and I crammed and wrote papers when I should have been sleeping. I knew very few people in my new town, and in a very real way, Bruno was my best friend.

Since that day I got him more than twenty years ago, my life has changed many times over. I've moved several more times and worked many different jobs, some of them in completely new fields. I moved from subject-matter expert into management, proficient doer into learning-as-I-go leader. I've become a father, twice. I've experienced losses. And I've had many more pets. But Bruno remains the one that changed the way I think.

No experience in life is regrettable if we learn from it; this is even more true if we help others learn from it, too.

Bruno may have been a secondhand dog, but he was a top-notch teacher. I learned from him and want to help you learn, too. In the next eight sections, I will share the lessons he taught me.

Bruno hears a bag of chips opening.

Lesson 1: Focus on what's important.

Bruno and I would play all of the time. Play consisted of me throwing a toy and Bruno retrieving it. Bruno had three favorites: a racquetball, a squeaky barbell, and Little Caesar. Bruno would become obsessed with these mouth-sized little friends of his. Once he would retrieve a plaything, he would drop it next to me, and then his stare would go from me to the toy, back and forth, until I threw it again. This would go on ad infinitum.

The problem with his playing is that he would shut out everything else in his life: eating, drinking, or relieving himself. His entire four-pound frame would stand on red alert as he stared at the toy. Sometimes I would be reading a book on the couch, and I would get this weird feeling. I'd look around the room, and you know what I'd see? Crazy Bruno, staring at his toy and then back to me. The intensity of his gaze was like getting hit with a spitball. You could ignore it for a while if you were concentrating on something, but eventually the annoyance broke through and it had to be dealt with.

I dealt with it by putting his toys up and out of reach when we were done playing. Or at least when I was done playing with him, because Bruno was never done playing.

One morning after leaving for work, I got a few miles away before realizing that I had forgotten something. I returned home and walked towards the house. I started wondering: *What does Bruno do all day at home? Watch TV? Jump on the bed?* These thoughts amused me, so I walked quietly up to a window and looked inside.

Bruno stood rigid like a macabre taxidermy project. His whole being was locked on a toy, his barbell, which I had forgotten to put away.

As an experiment, I didn't pick up the toy when I left the house. I popped home at lunchtime, and peered in the window. Bruno was now seated and his eyes were droopy, but his nose was an inch from his toy. He hadn't moved. I left the toy in place again, and returned to work. When I got home at the end of the day, Bruno's eyes were closed, and his head was on top of the toy. And he was still in the same place he was when I had said goodbye ten hours before.

Having the ability to fixate on a single purpose is necessary for some animals to exist. Imagine a lioness stalking a gazelle in the tall grass. Just before initiating the pounce to bring down dinner, she gets distracted, "Oh look! That cloud looks like a teddy bear!" The gazelle disappears; the lioness goes hungry.

Dogs tend to have a little obsessive-compulsive disorder. Bruno was their king due to his superior level of this disorder. It was admirable to see how he could focus on one thing tirelessly while shutting out the rest of the world.

In graduate school, I was attending class in the morning, working in the afternoon, and then conducting research and writing my thesis in the evening. Each one of these activities took focus and concentration. I couldn't worry about studying at work; I couldn't worry about work when writing my thesis. I learned to be more like Bruno, to focus on the task at hand and to shut out other distractions and worries.

Years later, I took a position as a management development specialist in the human resources department of a large corporation. I was hired because of my background in clinical psychology and my ability to apply behavioral principles in a corporate setting. My first project was within operations where I served as the human resources liaison to the business.

The problem I was asked to evaluate was attrition. Over the previous few years, the organization had moved from a centralized structure to having several remote, decentralized regional offices. A recent merger in another state coupled with explosive customer growth meant the company was opening new offices very quickly. While technology and processes are relatively easy for a company to replicate and relocate, culture is not simple to export. As a result, we found ourselves with skyrocketing attrition rates in our new offices, reaching nearly fifty percent in some job families.

The HR department's solution was to start providing retention bonuses. Customer service representatives, the group experiencing the most turnover, would receive a sizable bonus for each quarter they worked, and then another larger bonus if they stayed for four quarters. Human resources determined from an exit interview form that the reason that employees were leaving was FNJ: Found New Job. According to local management, employees said they were leaving for other positions that paid more money for easier work. More money thus seemed like a viable solution, at first blush.

I, however, didn't agree with that assessment. I had developed and delivered training to the management teams in each office, and spent a lot of time observing each work environment. I suspected that Found New Job was not a cause for attrition, but rather a destination for our exiting employees, and the simplest excuse to put on an exit interview. My problem was: How do I get to the root cause before we institute a stay-bonus program that might be a waste of money?

I told my boss my concerns about the retention bonus. I asked if instead of rubber-stamping the "answer," I could take some time to validate the true cause. He gave me two weeks to develop and implement a fact-finding process to find the cause of attrition.

What have I done? Where does one begin something like this?

Bruno may have been a secondhand dog, but he had laser-beam focus. I needed to apply that focus on this problem.

I couldn't go in with opinions. I needed facts. So I developed survey questions for employees who had already left the company. I asked around about how to implement this survey and was told: *Use a simple SAS business analytics mainframe tool to crunch the data.* There were about five words in that answer that I understood. All of the others were completely alien to me.

I should explain that while others in college were taking computer programming, I was studying classical poetry; while some were learning computer languages, I was trying not to fail French. I did take accounting one semester. The final project in that class was to balance the books of some fictitious company for a calendar year.

I was $0.52 off. I taped two quarters and two pennies to the page. The professor gave me a C for creativity and requested a return promise from me NOT to take any more classes he taught. Accounting was not my calling.

WWBD? I asked myself. *What would Bruno do?* I knew what he would do. He would bring his laser-beam focus to this challenge.

I worked obscene hours. I called people from around the company, the pocket-protector types that normally would have no contact with me in my role, and asked questions about tools and metrics. My dad, a computer guru from the early days, spent hours teaching me SAS and mainframe basics. I worked with my HR colleagues to get a list of all employees who had voluntarily left the company over the past two years. I refined the survey so I could get to the bottom of the attrition issue.

One week after I started, I had a process, a survey, names and phone numbers of the people I needed to interview, and enough SAS and mainframe knowledge to be proven right or wrong in a short period of time.

I can't say I had anything that resembled balance during that time. I'm sure I wore clothes, but looked like I slept in them. Because I had. I'm sure I ate, but it was at my desk or on the run. I'm sure I went home to shower, but was a ghost to my family.

That's what it means to be focused. Most people can do many things fairly well, but not all at the same time. Maybe we can have it all, just not all at once.

- Want to have an incredible beach body? Give up many of the foods you like.
- Want to be a competitive eater? Give up abs of steel.
- Want to wear designer clothes, drive a sports car, and purchase every new toy on the market…on an entry level salary? Give up trying to retire young.
- Want to quit working at 50? Give up spending money like a drunken sailor on shore leave.
- Want to graduate summa cum laude? Give up hopes of winning the coveted Beer Pong trophy.

- 🐾 Want to take that job in the city? Give up the quiet life you have built for yourself in the country.
- 🐾 Want to take that first promotion into management? Give up being rewarded for being a subject-matter expert.
- 🐾 Want to build a reputation for being the "go to" at work? Give up your nine-to-five mindset.
- 🐾 Want to have a couple of children? Give up going on spontaneous road trips with your buddies in the middle of the night.
- 🐾 Want to leave your mark, be the best at what you do, compete at the top level in your field? Give up everything that doesn't take you closer to your goal.

On the flip side, you can always settle for average. And the good news is that you don't have to give up anything.

Michelangelo would have described his ability to sculpt like this: *"Want to turn a block of marble into an angel? Give up the pieces of marble that aren't part of the angel."*

About what are you single-minded? Bruno was single-minded about his toys. Young kids are often single-minded about their BFFs or sports. As we get older, our focus usually shifts to our jobs, our significant others, our children.

Do you define yourself exclusively by the object of your focus? Many successful people do this, but it comes at a price. The greatest risk is losing it all. What happens to you if your entire identity is wrapped up in what you do and on what you focus? Mark Twain cautioned against the judiciousness of this when he wrote: *"Put all of your eggs in one basket and then watch that basket."* Consider these unfortunately common scenarios:

- 🐾 The athlete whose injury makes future competition impossible
- 🐾 The billionaire whose fortunes are lost overnight
- 🐾 The mom who's becoming an empty-nester
- 🐾 The woman who's single again after thirty years of marriage

When I was trying to resolve the attrition issue at work, I was not able to demonstrate balance. I was the very picture of single-mindedness and focus. Sometimes it is necessary to be very focused for a short duration in order to get a desired result. Note: **You can keep**

that pace going for a sprint, but not a marathon.

It is far better to strive to accomplish balance in our roles than settle for all-or-nothing within a single identity or role. It is safer, too.

The consequence of not being able to bring single-mindedness to what is in front of you is equally perilous. Do you remember being told when you were young, *"These are the best days of your life?"* I'm glad that was a lie. Those were difficult times. Teenagers are master jugglers. They need to meet the needs of their social circles, academic advisors, individual teachers, parents, jobs, and self. No, those are not the best days, but they are critical days for learning lessons about living a balanced life. Imagine a teenager who focuses on social obligations only. School work suffers. Or academics only. Relationships suffer. Rather than being all-or-nothing, it's better to focus on the task at hand, finish it completely, and then move on to the next thing.

Success is found in single-mindedness and focus on whatever it is that lies in front of you at a given moment in time. Yes, contentment and happiness are found more readily when you have a measure of passion about what is at hand. The key is balance, just like in the food pyramid. Things that you must do, but that bring you little joy, should be treated like work. Sometimes we have unrealistic expectations about what we should receive from work. We are paid to do it instead of having to pay others for the opportunity to do it. Shouldn't that tell us something? Things we do for work, but things that do not necessarily thrill us, should be done well, quickly, immediately, and for as long as is necessary to reach our goals.

As for the things that bring us joy, they are like ice cream. Perhaps ice cream should be considered a rare treat instead of a daily staple of our diets. By making it rare, we don't grow tired of it, and we don't take it for granted. What is the best way to enjoy something we are excited about? It should be savored slowly and fully, with a sense of passionate awareness at all times. We give it our full attention because we are enraptured and delighted.

Author Mark Sanborn suggests this: *"Each day do two things: do one thing for the pure fun of it and the other thing because it is difficult and will make you a better person."*

It is never hard to wake up a child on Christmas morning. Do you have the ability to spring out of bed like a child at Christmas when you are facing a loathsome task? How you perform in those circumstances defines your character.

You will put on and take off many hats throughout your lifetime. By thinking through the legacy you want to leave and the essential behaviors required to accomplish that mission, your success becomes more likely.

1. What are the various roles you play in your life right now that you consider important to your happiness? Fill in your answer under the **ROLE** heading.

ROLE	RANK	KEY WORD(S)	BEHAVIORS THAT SHOW IT

2. Go back and rank the importance of the roles from most important (1) to lesser importance (7) under the **RANK** heading. Don't worry if you don't have seven on your list, and don't get hung up on trying to nitpick items that are too hard to rank.

3. Spend a minute to reflect on the legacy that you want to leave for each role you listed. Come up with one or two **KEY WORDS** describing how you most want to be remembered, and then write those in the blank.

4. Thinking about the key words you listed, take it to the next level by writing some descriptive ways that you can adopt **BEHAVIORS THAT SHOW IT.** In other words, how can you show those who see you in any given role that you are committed to excellence when you are with them?

Here is an example of what this might look like for me:

ROLE	RANK	KEYWORD(S)	BEHAVIORS THAT SHOW IT
Father	1	Listen	Establish eye contact when talking with kids; keep eyes on them; reflect what they say to me to verify understanding; delay asking follow-up questions until they are done talking; etc.
		Role Model	Eliminate behaviors that I do not wish to see in them (e.g., quit smoking on 02/08); eat balanced food and meals; invite them to exercise with me; be a courteous driver; etc.

— For the purpose of illustration, I give some examples of **KEY WORDS** and **BEHAVIORS** that might be a struggle for me to **SHOW** consistently. By writing them down, it makes them real and specific to me; it also allows me to ask the "audience," in this case my kids, to tell me how I am doing on these items.

5. Pick a couple of items from the **BEHAVIORS THAT SHOW IT** column, for the role that you ranked #1. Put those behaviors into practice for a couple of days every time you have an opportunity to do so. Write down in the margin the following information:

🐾 What did you do specifically?
🐾 What reaction did you receive?
🐾 How did it make you feel?

Bruno could bring focus to what was important to him. Can you? Bruno was a dog and, as such, he wasn't very good at living a life of balance. *Are you?*

Bruno demonstrates OCD.

Lesson 2: Ask for help.

One night, Bruno woke me up by making a pathetic yelp. I flipped on the light, and ran to where he was lying in his cage. He had snagged his dew claw on his bedding, and it was pulling the nail at a bad angle and causing him terrible pain. He wasn't very cooperative when I tried to help him, but at least he wasn't biting me. Finally, I freed the claw and he licked his foot for a minute to take away the pain. And then he licked my hand, as a sort of canine thank you.

He needed me and wasn't too proud to ask for help.

Another time the house was VERY cold during a winter night. Cash was tight which meant doing without a lot of things. Heat was one of those things. I kept the thermostat very low, despite all the promises that I'd made to myself as a child to rebel against my parents' habits.

In the middle of the night, I felt this scratching by my pillow. From the red glow of my alarm clock, I could see Bruno standing next to my head, and he was dragging one paw on the pillow in front of my face. This was a quiet gesture, but it had specific meaning. "Let. Me. In." I lifted up the covers, and Bruno ducked underneath. He forced his way to the foot of the bed, completed a couple of circles, and then plopped down against my toes. He was still there when I woke up the next morning.

The poor little guy was freezing. He needed help. He wasn't afraid to ask.

Asking for help has never been easy for me. Perhaps it's pride or an overdeveloped desire to be self-sufficient. But there have been things that I couldn't do myself, and I would continue failing in my efforts to accomplish until I got some help.

At the time, I was a family therapist, and was struggling with one boy on my caseload. I couldn't seem to break through the walls he had built around himself. I tried everything, and nothing worked. I was getting discouraged and, worse yet, I was getting frustrated with the boy.

Finally, having nothing to lose, I called my boss and asked for help. My boss served as my counselor. His actual role was to counsel counselors. I laid out the situation for him, ending with letting him know how frustrated I was getting. By the end of the call, I had several suggestions that he had given me to try.

Guess what? The first suggestion I tried worked. As a result, in a short period of time, the boy was doing better and lowering his barriers, and I was feeling fresh instead of frustrated. It got easier to ask for help after that.

Years later, I was struggling to develop a process that would enable me to determine why employees were quitting. I had created a survey, I had a list of 273 names and phone numbers, and I had learned a little bit about SAS and using the mainframe. But I lacked time to make 273 calls, enter data, and get empirical outcomes.

Bruno may have been a secondhand dog, but he understood that his standing in the family entitled him to ask for and receive help when he needed it. I may have been a new employee, but being part of the human resources family gave me the right to ask for and receive help.

Quite a few things were working against me.

Time, for example, was very short. I needed outcomes--not just volunteers--in one week. I couldn't just let people answer my request for help with a wishy-washy, "We'll see." I needed firm commitments of their support and time.

Timing was another problem. I needed help during the week of Halloween. Most of the people I worked with in human resources treated Halloween like Wiccan priests and priestesses...like it was a sacred holiday. And since the people we would be calling at home told us that they were leaving our company for other nine-to-five jobs, we needed to call them during the evening hours. Yuck! I was asking my colleagues to give up some time with their families in the evening to help me--during a holiday.

My final obstacle to making this task easy is that I had nothing to offer my colleagues as an enticement to help me out, no pouch of Scooby snacks. I was new, and I was a grunt. Not the best combination for luring people to stand in line and offer assistance.

On the other hand, I had little to lose. I wasn't going through this process because it benefited me personally. It was the right thing to do, a little due diligence before spending corporate funds. And the only downside I could come up with was that I could be rejected.

So I asked. I sent out emails to coworkers in my own department since I knew their names. Then I walked the floor and talked to anyone who looked like an HR employee. I explained what I needed to accomplish. I apologized for the short notice and the holiday. Business opportunities and challenges don't always appear around holes in our personal schedules. I outlined the process. I sold the benefits, obtaining firsthand information from our internal customers. And then I begged for help.

And I got it. I got enough volunteers to conduct all of the telephone interviews with time to spare.

Why don't we always get the help we need? There are two main reasons why we don't get help. Either we don't ask for help, or we ask when we should be doing things for ourselves.

Why do we sometimes struggle to ask for help? One reason is fear. What if we were to ask for help, and no one jumped in? What are we afraid of? Rejection can be a powerful behavior modifier. Remember the kid at the park who was picked last to play kickball? This happened to him several times. It hurt each time, with no reduction in pain for his increased sense of alienation and rejection. Eventually, he convinced himself, *Kickball is stupid. I hate kickball. I don't want to play anyway.* Standing in the lineup while teams were picked made the boy vulnerable. Being picked last caused a feeling of rejection. How did he control his rejection? He stopped being vulnerable; he stopped giving others the chance to reject him.

Another reason we fail to ask has to do with unconscious selfishness. "Be beholden to no man" is something I observed from a close friend growing up. This friend would give the shirt off his back to anyone in need. One time as a young adult, I was sitting at the kitchen table visiting this friend when there was a knock at the door. He answered it. I heard some talking but couldn't make out the words. After a few moments, he came into the kitchen and took his wallet off the counter. He came back into the kitchen a minute later, and I asked him what was going on with the person at the door.

"The guy at the door says he lives around the corner and just got home from work. When he got in, there was a message on his machine from the hospital. His wife's appendix burst, and she was rushed to the ER. He ran out of gas right down the block, and was in such a hurry to get to the hospital that he left with his wallet and house keys locked in the house. He asked for a few bucks to get enough gasoline in the gas can in his trunk so he could make it to the hospital. So I gave him $20."

That whole story is crap, I said. *You know that, right?*

"Probably," he said undisturbed. "I know I won't see that money again."

So, um, why did you do it?

"I would rather give him the money with a ninety-nine percent chance that he's lying than not give him the money and then worry all night that he was telling the truth. I'd want someone to believe me and help me if I needed it."

This was not a rare occurrence on this friend's part. He is the most generous person I know, bar none. But he never asks others for help. He would rather do without or do it himself than to trouble anyone with something he needs.

So why do I say that is linked to unconscious selfishness? Not letting others help you is selfishness because it deprives them of the good feeling that comes with giving. My friend gave to that man, and felt good about doing it. But his not asking me or even letting me help him throughout the years deprives me of the great feeling I would have gotten from giving to him.

I understand how important it is for people to have that feeling they get when they give. Now, when my kids ask me what I want for my birthday or Christmas, I don't say, "I just want good kids." My mom used to say that, and it drove me crazy. At some point I replied to her, "Okay, that's not going to happen. What's your second choice?" I no longer deprive my children of the joy of giving. Now I tell my kids what they can get me for a special holiday because I know how important it is for them to give and receive that good feeling they get from giving.

Sometimes we don't get help because all we do is ask others for help. Asking too often can come across as us being lazy or afraid to fail. My son asked me the other day if I would send out his sister to help him haul firewood. I was able to answer him promptly and passionately: "No! That is YOUR job; your sister is doing HER job." His job was not too difficult or complicated. He was just being like all kids can be: lazy.

Other times, we ask for help too often because we are afraid that we will fail if we do it ourselves. Yes, we will fail. Don't even question that. Few people do something perfectly on their first attempt.

Many years ago, I went to a class that taught home maintenance basics, things like how to change out a ballcock in the toilet and how to change a light switch. Armed with a little knowledge, I determined that I would tackle the toilet after church one Sunday. I had the tools laid out, the new parts to replace the old ones, and an afternoon to get this five-minute repair done. *What could go wrong?*

Apparently, the practice toilet in class had never been filled with liquid; in fact, it had never had a real, live pressurized water pipe attached to it before. And sadly, the real-world toilet in front of me was full of water and attached to a fire hose--that snapped off in my hands in the ON POSITION seconds into the repair. I had water under considerable pressure spraying in all directions, soaking me and turning the bathroom into a swimming pool within minutes.

In hindsight, conducting this repair on a Sunday--when the nearest open store was a ninety-minute round-trip--was less than prudent on my part. By the time I returned from the store with the parts required to TURN OFF THE WATER, there was not a dry cloth in my house. My wife had to build a clothes-dam to keep the river from overflowing its banks and filling the living room.

I failed at that little repair, a failure that was as foreseeable as it was spectacular. But I was getting over my fear of failure in a big way.

Do you need help with something in your life? If it's something important, something you can't take care of yourself, and something that has a significant amount resting on it, ask. Bruno couldn't untangle his claw or keep warm on his own. Both were important enough for him to seek help. Be more like Bruno.

Do you need help with something in your life, but are too proud to ask for help? What parent would be mad at a toddler for saying, "Mom, I'm hungry!" In toddler-ese, that's asking for help, a request for food (specifically Cheetos and cookies if your kids are like mine were). Put away your pride by knowing that those who care about you and share common goals with you want to see you succeed. They want and wait to help you. You honor them by giving them an opportunity to do something for you.

Do you want help with something, but it's something you can and should do yourself? Don't play Tom Sawyer by trying to get others to do your work for you. Do the work yourself. It builds your character and strengthens your resilience. Are you afraid to do something yourself because you're afraid you will fail? Get over it. You probably will fail initially. In the end, it's not the success you receive for your effort that matters, but rather what you learned from your effort that makes the difference. Plus, your odds of failing the second time are much lower. Get the first time out of the way.

Here are some ways to **determine if you should ask for help.** Ask yourself these questions:

- Do you have little or no experience with what you are trying to accomplish?
- Do you consider the consequence of failure huge (i.e., risk of life or health, costly repairs, missed deadline for important project, etc.)?

If you answer **yes** to either question, you might consider putting aside your fear or pride, and asking for help.

Here are some ways you can **determine if you should do it yourself.** Ask yourself these questions:

- Is this something that might be difficult for you to accomplish but not impossible?
- Is the consequence of failure inconsequential (i.e., inconvenience, petty embarrassment, or a story you will laugh about in the near future)?

If you answer **yes** to either question, stop looking for excuses or being lazy. Jump in.

1. For some things in your life, you should ask for help. Other things you should do for yourself. Take a minute to think about situations that you've faced or are facing currently where you were unclear if you should ask for help or do it on your own. Write down a few of those items in the space provided.

I SHOULD ASK FOR HELP	I SHOULD DO MYSELF

2. Go back to your list above. Find an item on the **I SHOULD ASK FOR HELP** column that is a current situation you are facing. Put a star next to the item you can now commit to asking for help in accomplishing. Then go back to an item on the **I SHOULD DO MYSELF** column that you've been putting off. Put a star next to the item you now commit to trying to tackle on your own without excuse.

3. After completing your starred items, write in the margin a brief description that includes:

For I SHOULD ASK FOR HELP

🐾 Who did you ask for help?
🐾 What was holding you back from asking (i.e., fear, pride, other)?
🐾 What was the outcome?
🐾 Would you ask for help again given the outcome?

For I SHOULD DO IT MYSELF

🐾 What was the outcome?
🐾 Would you try something like this again given the outcome?

Bruno wasn't afraid to ask for help when it mattered most. And he wasn't afraid to get the toy himself when he could.

Lesson 3: Really listen.

 Bruno was the size of a deflated football. To say his bladder approximated a lentil bean was not much of an exaggeration. He needed to go out regularly and frequently. But when we were busy, we would forget about him. Bruno, the poor little guy, was sometimes left dancing around for a while, crossing and re-crossing his legs, and making a number of laps between me to the outside door.

One night while I was studying at home, Bruno was barking in the background. I was later told that he had been barking for a while. I didn't hear it. I was focused on something else.

After several minutes, my wife asked me what was wrong with Bruno.

"He's. A. Dog!" I yelled back, as if that explained everything. I listened for a bit, and sure enough Bruno was barking somewhere in the house. I ignored him for as long as I could. Finally, the barking stopped. Somehow, this made me more concerned than when he had been barking. I got up to check.

Bruno was sitting by the back door with his head down and ears back. Next to him was a very large pee spot. The poor little guy had done everything he could to get help. He raised up his little voice but to no avail. I couldn't be mad at him. This stain on the floor was my fault. I hadn't really listened.

Bruno knew how to really listen. Every night when I would drive up to the house, his ears would perk up, and I would see him silently barking at me from the front window. We shared a driveway with another home. Cars were always coming and going. When he heard a car, his radar-dish ears would go up, but he would only react by barking and getting up when he heard my car.

Bruno had attuned his ears to listen, not just hear.

This is something I try to put into practice every day. When I worked with kids, sometimes I would see some extreme reaction or blow up. Afterwards, I would look for signs that I had missed to see if there was something I had overlooked due to not listening. My children would bust me for this when they were young. My then three-year-old son said: "Daddy, I want you to listen to me with your eyes." Even at three, he could tell the difference between listening and LISTENING.

Fast forward to my HR days when I was calling former employees to ask them about their experience with our company. Listening took on a whole new meaning. I had an agenda, and a list of questions and decision trees wherein a former employee's answer to Question A would guide me to which Question B to ask.

Before making my first call, I closed my office door and paced. I practiced my opening statement, the statement that would make the person on the other end want to talk to me. I wrote little cheats on my white board. I anticipated every possible answer.

Bruno may have been a secondhand dog, but he was a world-class listener.

It is hard to listen without bias and enter what might be a difficult conversation without having some predetermined conclusions drawn. I was entering this exit interview process with a bias AND predetermined conclusions. That was how I conducted my planning phase. I had constructed tidy little flow charts and boxes to enter in the data I was sure that I would receive. I had done thorough research so I would have both qualitative yet quantifiable answers to the attrition riddle.

I wish I had spent less time preparing the process and more time practicing emotive, reflective listening. Sadly, I entered into this process thinking of these individuals as puzzles to be solved instead of people to be heard, cared for, and valued.

I used my opener, secured their willingness to help me, and asked my first question. And I rarely got beyond that first question. People had things they wanted to say and share. They wanted to be heard. There were some things that had bothered them for a long time that they needed to unload. Apparently, some of our offices weren't just a bad place to work; some of them were toxic.

Here are some of the most memorable things I heard:

- It was a sweatshop with air conditioning.
- If only they treated us like we were human...
- The supervisors were so mean. I would cry all the way to work, and all the way home from work each day.
- I promised my husband that I wouldn't talk about this any longer.
- When I was working there, I was so upset and stressed out that it nearly ruined my marriage.
- When I voiced my concerns, I was told, "You can be replaced tomorrow."
- I wouldn't have stayed for any amount of money.

My original intent was to ask questions and document responses. But I ended up playing therapist and counselor. I couldn't follow my own agenda; I had to go with theirs.

What kind of listener are you? When someone is talking to you, are you giving your full focus to what the speaker is saying? Or are you thinking about what you are going to say next?

Here's a secret I learned as a family therapist, a role where building rapport was essential. If you want to be viewed as a good conversationalist and listener, let the other person do most of the talking. Find ways to dig deeper, keep him talking, and ask follow-up questions. Not only will you hear some very interesting things that may be helpful diagnostically, but you also will be viewed as more compassionate.

There are many reasons we don't really listen. The most common is that we think we are better at multitasking than we are in actuality. Many states have passed laws making it illegal to talk on a cell phone without a speakerphone feature while driving. This was done to counter the many car accidents caused by distracted drivers fumbling with phones while driving. Newer research indicates that these "hands-free" laws will have little effect in lowering accidents. The reason: Conversation takes concentration. Talking to someone on the phone, with or without wires and with or without using your hands, requires mental effort that takes attention away from the act of driving. Drivers think they can drive and carry on a phone conversation well--until they rear end the car in front of them.

How listening has been modeled for us has a big impact on how we listen to others. Manners, both good and bad, are taught. Good listening shows good manners; poor listening shows poor manners. I know from my personal experience as a parent that really listening, listening with my mind and eyes, takes a lot of effort. From corporate America, I have heard amazing stories about the kind of things a boss would do when meeting one on one with an employee in his office. Taking phone calls, clipping finger nails, checking email. These are just a few. What kind of message does that send to the person across the desk? Guess what? These were some of the things I heard from employees who had quit their jobs citing "poor management" as the cause.

What can you do to get better? First, you have to know how your behavior is perceived. I worked with a vice president who had legendary intolerance for tardiness. One time, I came to a meeting of his five minutes late. He looked up as I entered and said, "If I wanted the meeting to start at 8:35, I would have scheduled it for 8:35 instead of 8:30." Guess whose meetings I was never late to again? Years later when we became friends, I asked him about this "quirk" of his. He told me this: "I've always hated it when someone thinks that his time is more important than the time of a room full of others." It was about respect. Showing up late to his meetings showed disrespect.

Likewise, not really listening shows disrespect to the person speaking. If you force yourself to view poor listening as disrespectful, it will help prompt you to do better when your attention begins to sway.

Another way to improve is to consciously restate what the person is saying in your mind. Pretend there is going to be a quiz, and you are cramming. It's imperative that you pack in as much during this cramming session as you can if you are to do well on the test. Guess what? When you are replaying what was just said, you won't likely have the extra attention span to be thinking about what you're going to say next!

You know yourself well, and you understand your listening habits and patterns.

1. Take a minute to reflect on the things that you do when you should be listening to others. Since most people spend the majority of their time at home or at work, I'm targeting those two places for you to list your I'm-not-really-listening behaviors.

AT HOME I TEND TO...	AT WORK I TEND TO...

Want to improve? Make it cost you something.

Years ago, I consulted with a director who was frustrated by one of her manager's habits of interrupting his team members when he should have been listening. I partnered with this manager who told me that he wasn't even aware of this problem. So here's what we did:

🐾 Told his team that he wants help in improving this issue.
🐾 Placed a bell, the kind you find at hotel counters to summon a bellman, on the edge of his desk.
🐾 Asked team members to ring the bell if he interrupted them.

Sounds brutal, right? It was. Guess what? Those simple steps made the bad behavior stop overnight. Why? The manager was now made fully aware of his behavior, and he worked very hard to NEVER hear that bell ring!

2. Here's my challenge to you. If you are serious about eliminating those behaviors you listed above, do this:

- 🐾 Tell your family and your colleagues what you are trying to accomplish.
- 🐾 Ask them to make you aware of your behavior if you were to slip into non-listening behaviors.
- 🐾 Put $1 in a manners bank whenever you are caught slipping.

3. Want to add real punishment to your behavior? Give all of the money you raised in bad behavior fines to the political party you disagree with most.

Bruno didn't need help listening. He was a natural-born listener. While he didn't have an extensive vocabulary, he would tune into key words like cookie, toy, ball, walk, outside, and bed. Because he could never be sure under what context or situation these words might appear, he kept his ears in constant tune for those key, musical words that he longed to hear. Try it. Be like Bruno.

52

Lesson 4: Do the right thing.

Bruno eventually got married. At least that's the way I like to look at it. Bruno liked to look at it differently: "Who let that wench in my house?" Milo (I know it's a boy's name) came and joined our family a few years after Bruno. She was a puppy, and grew quickly. Bruno was slow to warm up to her. During the first six months, I would have to separate them because Bruno would get mean and pounce on Milo. After about six months, though, Milo was bigger than Bruno. Bruno backed off.

Like a good older brother or spouse, Bruno grew fiercely protective of Milo. One evening, I got a ride home from a friend. Since the driveway was on an angle high above the house, I couldn't see that both dogs were playing in the front yard that night when I approached. Not recognizing the sound of the car, Bruno went on alert. As I started down the steep steps, I could hear both dogs start barking. Milo's lower voice was getting more distant; Bruno's higher voice was getting louder and louder. Before my eyes could adjust to the darkness, Bruno was a few feet from me--barking, growling, and threatening to pounce on me, the evil intruder.

I doubt that Bruno was actually trying to protect Milo. Milo was a chicken-heart, but she never needed protection. Her strategy was to outrun anything that scared her! I think Bruno charged because of little-man syndrome. He tried to overcompensate for being tiny by being more aggressive and fierce.

In my mind, I like to think that he was being strong, acting on the convictions of his character. This was his yard. He was the alpha dog. Having a marked, well-defined territory is important to many animals. More than once, the neighbors' cat would sleep near our front porch, and Bruno would chase her into a tree. The cat was significantly bigger than Bruno. But Bruno was going to stand up for what was right, even if he got his eyes scratched out.

Another time, Bruno took on a bigger challenge. Living in Upper Michigan, black bears were a constant reality. Especially in the springtime after hibernation, bears would be looking for food anywhere they could find it. I lived in the middle of hundreds of acres of wilderness. I had seen black bears within a stone's throw of my house while I sat outside sipping coffee. One morning, I found a pile of bear scat not twenty feet from my home. Unfortunately, Bruno got to it first. Instinct kicked in. Bruno rolled in it until he was covered completely in dung. Yelling would do no good (but trust me, I did yell and yell, and said some decidedly filthy things). His instinct told him what he had to do: mask his own scent in the smell of his enemy so that he could effectively stalk his predator without being noticed.

To cut the story short, no, I didn't allow Bruno to go stalk and kill the bear. But it was very hard to stop him. His programming was strong. I picked him up, much against my will, but his little legs kept pumping as if he were running. For the next several weeks, Bruno wasn't allowed outside without a leash. He would sniff the air, and I'm sure he was trying to find his arch enemy. He was not ready to back down from his mission.

I admired that determination. How many of us can face tough, nearly insurmountable obstacles without blinking? I had to push against some obstacles at work during that same time. I was working with a child, and I had a very different opinion of the appropriate treatment than his state-appointed caseworker held. This is typical, and it's not normally a problem. What made it a problem is that the child was going before the court, and both the caseworker and I were called to testify. My contract was funded through the state agency in which the caseworker was employed. To agree with him was polite and deferential to his wisdom and experience (thirty-two years on the job). Additionally, it would keep harmony...and hopefully funding...in the family. To disagree would be a problem.

I didn't back down when I testified. I disagreed as politely as I could. It was difficult. My relationship was never the same afterwards with that case worker. But I had done what I believed was right. And my funding was renewed.

Bruno could stand up naturally to opposition. He made it look easy. He showed me that I could do it, too, even if it took more out of me to do so.

Fast forward to my job in HR. I had a new problem as a result of the root cause I had uncovered. From all of the former employees my makeshift team had interviewed, I learned that no amount of money would have made these people stay with our company. The problem wasn't the job, it wasn't the pay, it wasn't the lure of a new job. The problem was poor management. Ouch.

How does a new employee go about breaking such news to a senior vice president? "Oh, you know that bonus you want us to pay? It's not going to do any good. People aren't leaving because of money. They are leaving because their managers suck..."

The announcement of the stay bonus was scheduled to go out the next morning from HR and the senior vice president of operations. I ran into my boss's office. "So what does that mean? Is it too late to stop the announcement? Can you get to Ray?" Ray was the senior vice president of operations, and the attrition was coming from within one area of his organization.

I was told that it was too late, but was praised for my diligence in pursuing this until I had true findings. My boss told me that he had tried to reach Ray, but he was gone for the day. I slumped back to my desk, discouraged.

A little bit later, I was talking to a work friend and mentioned that I was bummed because I had missed my opportunity to share some important information with the SVP of operations.

"How important is it?" he asked me.

"Very," I responded. "It's good news and bad news. But it's information he can use to make a bad situation good."

My friend told me, "If it's that important, go across the street to La Strada. He's having dinner with some of his vice presidents right now."

I was new, but I wasn't stupid. I needed to run this past my boss so I ran back into his office...to find that he was out for the day. Now I had a decision to make: Do I sit on this, or do I take matters into my own hands and buck protocol?

Bruno may have been a secondhand dog, but he had first-rate character.

Giddy up! We might be in for some rough riding!

I gathered my papers and thoughts, and headed across the street. When I got to the restaurant, I saw four people sitting around the table talking. One of them recognized me and waved me over. Once introductions were made, someone asked me if I needed something. I turned to Ray: "I came looking for you, Ray. I know that you don't know me from Adam, but..."

When I finished, Ray looked at my SAS report. Remember that I am no expert in reporting. I had a tenuous grasp on the data, but I knew the implications of what the report meant. Before I could attempt to give my sloppy, broken explanation of the data, Ray looked up at me and slapped the report with the back of his hand, "It's not about the money." He looked at his table mates, "It's that we treat people like crap."

I took a risk because I didn't know all of the right protocols, I had more passion than common sense, and I believed in what I was doing. Fortunately, Ray did too. A week later, he offered me a job reporting directly to him. My job was to fix the attrition problem by correcting the culture, rather than by buying "loyalty" with cash bonuses.

Doing the right thing. Character. Following the strength of your convictions. It's not easy, although some people make it look easy. Numerous people have demonstrated enormous courage in the face of opposition. There are religious martyrs such as St. Stephen, generally considered the first Christian martyr, who was stoned to death for his faith. Sir Thomas More was beheaded in 1535 because his religious belief would not allow him to approve of the divorce of King Henry the 8th. Some die for political convictions. Patriot Nathan Hale allegedly met the hangman's noose saying, "I only regret that I have but one life to give for my country." Mohandas Gandhi resisted tyranny through nonviolence and civil disobedience, but he was gunned down for his political positions. Years later, Dr. Martin Luther King, Jr., used similar nonviolent protest around social injustices, and that led to his assassination.

Standing up for what you believe does not mean you will automatically die the death of a martyr. In reality, trendsetters and trend-rebels stand up all of the time without doing anything noble or great, and it's no riskier than crossing a street. In the '80s, I'd see the blue or green-spiked-hair kids in the city. I was a kid too, and I thought it looked silly. *Should I pierce my eyebrow to be even more radical?* Whoops. That's been done now too. Just because something is bold or rebellious doesn't mean it merits making a stand. Make a stand when and where it counts.

Sometimes we are afraid to stand up because we don't want to stand out. A pre-teen is offered a cigarette by his friends. Even though he doesn't smoke, he takes one. Why? So he doesn't stand out. Think about a first date when your partner says: "I was thinking Chinese food for dinner. I love Chinese. Do you like Chinese food?" You say, "Sounds good." In reality, you would rather eat bark and pinecones than Chinese food. So why do you say sure? To get along. At work, your boss shares an idea with you about changing a work process, and she asks you for an opinion. You say, "Nice." It's the single most terrible idea you have ever heard. Why don't you stand up and say, "I'm not sure I see how that will make things better than what we have now. Am I missing something?" Why don't you disagree? You don't want to stand out, you don't want to make waves, you don't want to be perceived as different.

Leonardo da Vinci and Michelangelo were different. Einstein stood out. Thomas Edison was bold, as was the manufacturing maverick Henry Ford. Anne Sullivan and Helen Keller didn't follow convention. Nor did Joan of Arc.

1. You have certain character traits that "stand out," ones that are unique to you.

Write down **FIVE TRAITS THAT ARE UNIQUELY YOURS.**

5 TRAITS THAT ARE UNIQUELY MINE	ROLES WHERE I APPLY THOSE TRAITS

2. Next, refer back to your list of the various **ROLES** you play in your life. Fill in the **ROLES** that most closely corresponds with each trait you listed.

3. Hopefully, you discovered that you use those traits in nearly every role in your life. That is what differentiates a true character trait from something you can slip in and out of like a suit of clothes.

If you want to increase your effectiveness in each role you play, apply those traits you listed frequently, liberally, and continuously.

Sometimes we desire to fit in and fade into the background instead of stand out or take full advantage of our unique traits. The easiest way to blend in is to march in step with everyone else. For example, if your goal is to be ordinary at work, here are some pointers:

❧ Wear urban camouflage to work each day.
❧ Carry a venti coffee cup around with you at all times.
(Don't refer to it as large or extra large. Call it venti.)

* Use words like "synergies" in regular conversation.
* Do what you are asked to do.
* If you see that something is broken, do NOT fix it unless it is your job to fix it. And then only fix it when you are asked specifically to do it.
* Pace yourself based on the actions and speed of your coworkers.
* Get to work on time each morning, leave on time each evening, and take lunch at the same time--and for the full amount of time allotted--each day.

If you dare to stand out and do the right thing, there are no rules. And you don't need to be told what to do. Find a challenge or opportunity, and pursue it. You don't just do things because they are part of your day job or what you are paid to do. You do it because it's right, you do it because it's what drives you, and you do it because you know you can make a difference.

Bruno was driven by instinct that told him when to attack or stalk. He couldn't help himself. It was innate, a part of who he was. As a human being, you are guided less by instinct and more by choices. What character choice can you make today that will propel you into greater things?

Hate at first site -- Bruno meets Milo.

Lesson 5: Take risks.

Bruno was timid in many aspects of his life, but he was quite bold in others. He was particularly adventuresome around trying new foods. Once I left a bag of baby carrots open on the kitchen table. That's how I discovered that Bruno liked baby carrots. He had jumped on my chair, dragged the bag off the table, and then nibbled on every carrot before determining with certainty that yes, he did indeed like carrots.

Whenever a package crinkled, a can opener sounded, or a refrigerator light popped on, Bruno was there like a magic ghost with that "Whatcha got for me?" winning look on his face. In the fall, he wanted to be outside all the time. It didn't take me long to figure out why. He would stand under the apple tree and eat as much as he could before I caught him.

One time, I was sitting on the floor with a piece of candy a client had given me, something called a Warhead. The girl said that I should just pop the whole thing in my mouth. (Yes, I've lived this long because I accept blindly the suggestions of 14-year-olds. NOT!) Hearing the wrapper, Bruno appeared at my side with his winning look. *Okay*, I thought. *You want to be my food tester?* I held it out to Bruno. His pointy tongue eagerly probed the candy shell. He took several fast licks, probably afraid that I would pull it back from him. When he stopped licking, his face took on a sour look. And then amazingly, he returned to the candy and continued licking!

I have to be honest. I don't think I enjoyed that candy as much as Bruno did. But I did eat it. After that, I tried other things that Bruno enjoyed, like frog legs (except I didn't eat them raw or directly out of the lake).

So here I was, this lowly HR grunt, and the senior vice president of operations was offering me a job reporting directly to him! Ray's division made up more than sixty percent of the company. He had a small number of direct reports, and I couldn't imagine being in constant company with such an elite group.

This was an incredible offer, and I was thrilled, flattered...and scared to death. I called a friend of mine, someone I had been very close friends with since the third grade. I laid out the offer for him, outlining the key points. When I was finished, he asked, "So what's the dilemma? It sounds great."

The dilemma was fear. I could stay put and be a relatively big fish in a small pond. Or I could venture out into this huge ocean where I could fail miserably. I could picture ocean waves, an iceberg, and me.

My friend asked, "Scott, when have you ever failed at something that was important to you?" I thought for a bit. He had a point. I hadn't exactly failed in accounting. But it was true that I didn't like or care about the class, and my behavior and discipline around the work reflected that indifference. After a moment, he continued, "Go for it. You haven't failed, and you won't now either."

Bruno may have been a secondhand dog, but he was an intrepid explorer.

This job was out of my comfort zone. I knew nothing about operations. I was a good diagnostician and family therapist, but I wasn't sure that I knew anything about fixing a culture problem. There was a good chance that I would fail. My only comfort was that my failure would happen quickly and not be one of those drawn-out affairs wherein I would struggle and squirm for years before having a pillow put over my head while I slept.

I took the job. I could do it. Or die trying.

Some people are natural explorers and risk takers. They are driven by curiosity, a need to know how things work or what-would-happen-if-this thinking. These adventuresome personality types are likely reinforced when they are young and ripe for trying new things. As they continue to explore new things, they find new, bigger, better thrills, and this feeds even more adventures.

What keeps many people from taking more risks? Once again, fear rears its ugly head. I have a friend who was once lost in a bad part of town, and he drove around for miles until he found a familiar sign and got on the right road. Guess what? He won't go into unfamiliar surroundings without a GPS and a human navigator. One bad experience, and he is too fearful to try his luck again.

Others are unwilling to take risks because they have a false sense of security based on the status quo. They believe that if they don't rock the boat, the boat will not rock. Guess what? Waves come from all directions. You can sit like a statue and still be spilled over the side by a rogue wave.

How do you push yourself out of your comfort zone to try new things? First, ask yourself what is the worst that can happen if you take a risk and fail? Few jobs have decision-making power over life and death. Likely the worst that can happen is getting fired, losing money, or being wickedly embarrassed. These are not pleasant outcomes, but they also are not deadly.

Second, ask yourself what is the worst that can happen if you DON'T take a risk? At a place I worked, they offered certain employees the opportunity to take jobs in different departments. There was no pressure. Most chose to stay put in their current roles. Within a month, their jobs were eliminated and the jobs they had been offered had already been filled. They were less safe for not taking the leap into a new world.

Finally, actively challenge your aversion to take risks. Make it a point to try something new every day. Test a new restaurant or a new dish in an old restaurant, take a new way home, read a book in a new genre, start a new hobby, or watch a new TV show. Keep track of the pleasantness or unpleasantness of each new experience. When I was a kid, I hated mushrooms. My dad would say, "Good. More for me." At some point, I tried them. Guess what? I loved them! My dad no longer had the monopoly on the sautéed mushrooms after that point. Everything that is now familiar to you started off as a great unknown. Force yourself to try even more unknowns.

Fear can keep us from taking appropriate risks.

1. Take a minute to think about some risks that you considered taking in the past twelve months but avoided because the potential risk was too high or you were afraid of what might happen. Outline the **RISK** you didn't take.

THE RISK	WHAT STOPPED YOU	WORST CASE SCENARIO

2. Think about what you told yourself when you decided to pass on taking the risk. Take some time to think about your "self-talk" that contributed to your fear of taking that risk. Write it in the line **WHAT STOPPED YOU.**

3. Now that you have some distance from the situation, honestly evaluate what is the worst thing that could have happened had you taken a chance. Write that in the **WORST CASE SCENARIO** line.

Most of the things we fret about never come to pass. Much of the "self-talk" that takes place inside our heads is negative. It prevents us from taking chances. In that way, it prevents us from having new experiences, finding new favorite things, or growing from the occasional setback that is inevitable in life.

This reminds me of a story I read years ago. A man had recently buried his wife who passed during a sudden illness. He had a close friend with him while he went through his deceased wife's belongings in their marital home. In her underwear drawer, he found some lingerie they had purchased at an expensive store many years prior. He sat down on the bed with the lingerie, noting that the tags were still attached. The man then told his friend the story of where they were when they purchased it. He ended the story with this: She was saving this for a special occasion, maybe a trip to Europe or a nice weekend getaway. And that never happened. I wish she enjoyed them when she bought them instead of saving them for something "special" that never came.

How sad that many of us live in power save mode, conserving our energy, storing our most passionate dreams, or reserving our special china for a moment that might come too late for us to experience.

If a four-pound dog was willing to try licking an atomic warhead--more than once--imagine the limits that you can reach if you give yourself permission to live now instead of waiting for some mythical future day.

Lesson 6: Practice forgiveness.

 It's not easy being a dog. Especially a little one. Many dogs are empaths. They sense and absorb the emotions around them. There's the adage about the man having a terrible day at work where he's feeling kicked around, and he has nowhere to return the favor until he gets home. Then he kicks the dog.

More than once, I was not pleasant to Bruno's cheerful greeting. One time, I was much more than unpleasant. I was running late to work on a Saturday morning. I was late because I wanted pancakes for breakfast, and they took more time to make than I anticipated. I kept them warm in the microwave oven while I donned my coat and tie. Trying to multi-task, I plopped down on the couch with my plate and put on the week-end news. Bruno used his bionic senses to find the yummy scent. I was looking at the TV, not the dog. He had worked his way to the arm of the couch and was leaning over to my plate. Still unable to reach the food, he stretched his front legs forward and rested his paws on the edge of the plate. The plate cranked ninety degrees downwards. Pancakes, dog, and then syrup poured all over my clothes. I went nuts! I said some words that aren't printable. I may have thrown some pancake fragments.

Yeah, I lost it, and Bruno was the focal point of my explosion. He ran away and hid under the couch. The streak of syrup pointing the way ratted him out. I changed clothes and rushed out the door, still mad and worked up.

When I got home that night, I was calm. An hour into the day, I was able to laugh about it, and the people I told at work thought it was a hoot.

When I got home, Bruno met me at the door, tail wagging slowly.

We good? His eyes seemed to say.

"Yeah, we're good, Bruno. Sorry I lost it."

He followed me as I changed my clothes, stood under my feet while I made dinner, and plopped on my lap as soon as I sat down.

We all get mad or hurt. And we all need forgiveness. *Bruno wouldn't stay mad long, and he was quick to offer and accept forgiveness.*

Forgiveness is a lifelong lesson. A few years back, I stopped to get a haircut with my nine year-old son and eight year-old daughter. They didn't want to go inside, so I gave them the option to walk around or sit in the car while I hurried inside.

When I got back into the car, I smelled something VERY WRONG.

"I'm so sorry, Dad!" my son was saying. Long story short, he pushed in the cigarette lighter and tested its heat by placing it against the dashboard. The lighter won; the dashboard smoked and melted.

I had some....thoughts...about my son's actions. When we got home, I sent him to the garage and had him stand there without touching, or burning, anything. Standing on the driveway, my daughter voiced a concern: "Are you REALLY mad? Are you going to kill him?"

I was gratified to be able to tell her, "No, Alana, I'm not going to kill him. But I'm not happy. I think what he did was stupid and danger-ous." I paused, not sure if I should admit to her what I was about to say. "But Alana, as stupid as I think that was, neither one of you have come close to the STUPID things I had done by the time I was your age." I could tell that she was relieved. "But for now, let's just let Jack sweat it out a few more minutes in the garage."

Bruno, I wasn't able to react well when you spilled food all over me all of those years ago. But you'll be glad to know that I was able to learn your lesson by responding better when I forgave my son. I made it "all good" in the end.

The learning curve in my new role was steep. But I was getting the hang of things. While I was convinced initially that I didn't know what I was doing, I was getting things done. Attrition for customer service representatives went from thirty-eight percent to just over six percent in a few years. I instituted two-way communication teams to get the frontline employees involved and engaged in matters that involved them and their work. I started an employee survey that evaluated their perception of leadership. And I put a cash incentive on the improvement goal for the management effectiveness.

As time passed, my boss was promoted from senior vice president (SVP) of operations to the executive vice president (EVP) of internal operations. Instead of one division and sixty percent of the employees, Ray now was responsible for four divisions and eighty percent of the employees in the company. As his role expanded, so did mine. Attrition was under control in the operations division, so I turned my attention over to the other divisions that were new to Ray's leadership.

And it was while trying to make inroads within one of these new areas that I ran into a wall. I used the same approach I had always used in the past, but with leadership who didn't have experience working with me. I was the chief of staff of internal operations, and given my reporting relationship with Ray and proximity to him, everything I did was scrutinized. During one meeting with mid-level directors, I was trying to sell a concept that Ray and his direct reports had vetted in an earlier meeting. Rather than saying, "Ray said..." I tried to really sell the benefits of the approach. During the meeting, everyone was nods and grins. It seemed like we were all in agreement with this approach...

Until the next day. One of the participants left that meeting, sent an email to her SVP, and misrepresented EVERYTHING that I had said the day before. The SVP then forwarded the original message along with his scathing comments about my approach--an approach that I DID NOT TAKE--and sent it to two other SVPs and to Ray. Ray sent it to me with his comment: "Let's talk."

Never in the history of a relationship have the words let's talk been a promise of something good.

I went into Ray's office with my ears back but my teeth bared. I was embarrassed that Ray had been involved in something so petty. At the same time, my actions and words had been misrepresented. I was feeling angry and defensive.

I walked in to see that Ray was smiling. "Welcome to my world," he said. We talked about the entire situation. He listened, asked more questions, and finally settled back in his chair.

"This doesn't surprise me. What we are trying to do isn't going to be easy. You are the messenger of change. People don't always like change when it's pointed at them." I was gratified that we were on the same page. Then he surprised me. "You need to apologize to all of the SVPs for letting this get out of hand and for not involving them earlier in the discussion..."

My head spun around in a complete circle, and somewhere in the forest a tree toppled and crushed a mime. "Wait! You know that this..."

Ray was teaching me. One lesson was humility. He wasn't saying that I needed to be *taken down a notch* because I had misbehaved. He was teaching me that sometimes you need to lower yourself willingly in the eyes of others so that they can feel higher. Those SVPs had gotten riled up, and regardless of the accuracy of the reports that pushed their buttons, their finger was pointing at me. I needed to take a step back to them if I were to have any chance of working effectively with them in the future.

Another lesson was to accept responsibility for outcomes and not just actions. Apparently, the outcome of my meeting with the directors hadn't been as stellar as I thought it had been. I would have claimed a victory if things had gone well. Likewise, I needed to claim responsibility for the failure. Period.

Finally, Ray was reminding me of the power of asking for forgiveness. When you apologize for your actions to another person, you are laid flat. Most of the time, your apology not only will be accepted, but the person will minimize the offense.

After Ray and I talked, I went to the SVP who had helped stir the pot. Instead of going to him in anger and resentment, I simply apologized. I acknowledged that the outcome had gotten away from me, and that I should have handled this situation differently. His response? "It's no problem. I just thought we should all talk about it." What else could he do? Beat me? Call me an idiot? I had taken the step to clear the air, and all parties were now ready to move on.

A few weeks later, I was asked to give forgiveness by another. A couple of my best employees had broken a corporate policy, and I was told that they needed to be terminated. What happened was that I had emailed one of them the night before and asked him to get something for me in the morning. He didn't have what I needed on his computer, so he emailed another person who he knew had what I needed. Unfortunately, she had it, but wasn't going to be in until after I needed the document. The woman who had the document told her male co-worker her password so he could print the document. Faux pas. Exchanging passwords on private networks and work stations was forbidden.

By the time I got out of my meeting, one of my managers was waiting for me with my coat. That meant **LET'S GO WALK.** Once outside, she told me what happened, ending with the part about how the department that managed these kind of affairs said that termination was recommended. Intent versus Effect. The intent of these employees was to get me what I needed. They did not want to disappoint me. The effect was to break a corporate policy.

Once back in my office, I called that department. I made the case for ignorance on the part of my employees. I suggested that while this was a clear breach, the matter had been self reported immediately and it was a onetime thing. I begged for forgiveness on their behalf. The decision was left with me; I granted them mercy.

I called both of the employees into my office. Both had been crying. Before I could start, one of them said, "It's all my fault. I asked her for her password. She shouldn't be punished with me." The other employee argued just as much about why this was all her own fault instead of her co-worker's.

Once they finished, I raised up my hand like I had seen the Pope do. I crossed my hand in front of them both and said, "Your sins have been forgiven. Go and sin no more."

Guess which two employees became even more loyal?

Sometimes we need to be forgiven to clear the air. Other times we need to forgive for the same reason.

Bruno may have been a secondhand dog, but he was a forgiving friend.

Forgiveness is cathartic. When someone grants you forgiveness for a mistake, you feel lightened, unburdened. When you grant someone else forgiveness when he has wronged you, you feel fresh, like you're experiencing a new beginning.

Who do you need to forgive? This doesn't mean finding your junior year prom date who broke up with you at the dance and saying, "Hey, jerk-face. I forgive you for crushing me all of those years ago. I'm not going to let you hurt me any longer." First of all, that isn't offering forgiveness; it's venting and blaming. Second, it will cause you more hurt than healing.

Forgiving someone doesn't need to be done formally. It doesn't even need to be acknowledged by either party. It just means that you will not hold a particular slight or offense against the other person. You will not keep score. You will not bring it up. You will not act as if you have the moral upper hand in your future dealings with the other person.

Why does this matter? Holding a grudge creates bitterness. Prolonged bitterness and resentment change us. They serve no constructive purpose and may actually cause us physical harm. Some research even indicates that a bitter outlook on life can leach calcium from our bones and promote their brittleness.

Animals are capable of many characteristics, and when we love them, we tend to anthropomorphize them. But I believe the intentional, conscious ability to forgive is unique to mankind.

1. Who do you need to forgive?

Write in the **INITIALS OF THE PERSON** in the first column.

2. Finally, there is a place left for you to write the date you forgive the person. Forgiveness is a conscious choice. John F. Kennedy said, "Forgive your enemies but never forget their names." That is not true forgiveness because it is keeping score and making an effort to recall that you have been wronged.

Forgiveness is about choosing NOT to call the wrong into your memory. When you are ready to practice forgiveness, write in the **DATE FORGIVEN**. Writing in the date signifies that you are putting the memory of any wrongdoing in the past and that you hold that person blameless for anything they have done to you in the past.

INITIALS OF THE PERSON	DATE FORGIVEN

Do you need forgiveness? If you have any relationships in your life, you likely need regular forgiveness. Don't wait to clear the air. You will feel better, and they will feel better. If there's distance in any relationship in your life, ask yourself if there is a need to be forgiven or a need to extend forgiveness.

3. Of whom do you need to ask forgiveness?

INITIALS OF THE PERSON	DATE FORGIVEN

4. It feels great to clear the air. Once you've asked for forgiveness, write in the date.

5. In the margins, write down how it felt to say "I'm sorry" and to have a clean slate.

There's one more type of forgiveness that is necessary in order for us to grow and to move forward with our lives. We need to forgive ourselves.

Many of the people I counseled when I was a family therapist struggled because they couldn't get past the poor choices and mistakes they had made years before. These people lived in constant defeat, believing that they needed to be in a perpetual state of penance. This practice is self-defeating, and it leads to sabotaging happiness.

Sometimes people make decisions based solely on the information in front of them at the time when they must act. A three-year-old who is asked to choose between eating a Twinkie and eating a bowl of beets will not have to think long before shoving the Twinkie in his mouth. Is that a good decision from a health standpoint? Probably not. But the child is basing his choice on the information in front of him. In his limited experience, Twinkies are great, and beets are gross. He decides based solely on his current and limited information. He can't be faulted.

Other times, people understand the pros and cons of a particular decision, and they willfully choose the one that leads to grief. Thus, these people cannot claim ignorance for their flawed decision making. They are miserable, and they know it is their own fault.

In both cases, there is nothing to be gained by dwelling on mistakes or poor decisions. If your errors or bad decisions have hurt others along the way, seek forgiveness from them. As for yourself, it's time to grant yourself forgiveness so that you can move on. Acknowledge what you did and any harm it may have caused, and purpose to learn from that mistake and not repeat it. And while you cannot un-ring a bell, you can help others from making that same mistake.

Forgiveness is cathartic. Grant yourself the same forgiveness that you grant to others. And move on.

Bruno never went to church to repent, nor needed to. He understood that there was nothing to be gained by holding a grudge or waiting for someone else to take the first step towards restoration.

Once the syrup dried.

Lesson 7: Choose to be happy.

Bruno was usually happy. How do I know? Dogs have a language all their own. His eyes would get shiny, his ears would lean forward, his stubby tail would sing through the air. Returning home after a long day, I'd see all of that plus he would levitate three feet into the air until I picked him up so he could wipe his little pointy tongue all over my face.

One of my former managers told me that the most powerful advice I ever gave her was that when you're feeling down, you can pull yourself out of it by thanking or praising someone else. Why is it that when a couple is happy in a new relationship, they view every action of their partner as sweet, cute, or endearing? And when they're mad at that same person, all they can see is behavior that is annoying, stupid, and enduring? It's not that the behavior has changed as much as the person's attitude at that particular moment. When you are down, you tend to look for things that reinforce that mood. When you're up, you tend to have on rose-colored glasses.

When we first got Bruno, we were afraid to leave him out to free range during the day while we were gone. We thought he might get hurt since he was so little. My wife and I would fight about who would have to put Bruno into his cage as we left the house in the morning. Bruno would look so sad when we nudged him into his crate. Since most of his life had been spent inside that little box, we imagined that each time he was enclosed he would remember those sad, dark days when he would be locked up for days on end. Once we left the house, we would hear his cry coming from inside.

It broke our hearts.

One day, we didn't lock the cage all the way. Once we left, Bruno must have pushed against the door and made a break for it. We didn't have a Bruno-cam to know exactly what he had been doing all day long. But when I got home and went into the bedroom to let him out, he was yawning and blinking from a little doggie circle he had rolled himself into on my head pillow. He stood up, stretched, wagged his tail very quickly as if to say, "Thanks for letting me out of lock-up today!" And he licked my face like I had given him a side of bacon.

Bruno had survived his day on the lam. We never again locked him up when we left for work. His happiness each day when we returned was proof enough that we had made the right decision.

Being happy can be challenging at times. I don't mean faking it by slapping on a plastic smile to everyone around you. I mean choosing to be happy, showing happiness, and in turn spreading some happiness around.

As the chief of staff, I had to start letting go of the day-to-day responsibility for the cultural transformation and communication efforts that I used to manage. Ray had asked me to bring several communication departments into one as part of ongoing consolidation efforts. It had been very difficult work. Everyone had different ideas about how decisions should be made, who should move into what area, what job titles would be used, etc. Integration is hard work, and no matter how hard you try to keep people informed and happy, there will always be some who fight change.

On this particular day, I was heading to an off-site retreat with the newly consolidated communications team. This was the first time we had the whole team together, and the plan was to review goals, get to know each other, and create some common understandings to guide our work. I had just hired the director who was replacing me on the team. This was going to be bittersweet. I had hired half of these people and worked with some of them for more than thirteen years. Some of them were new to me, but I knew them by reputation to be very strong. And I was sorry that I would have less time to work with them.

A few miles into my drive, Ray called me. This was a call I had been dreading for some time. Ray was calling me to tell me that he was retiring. After more than thirty-five years in the organization, I was thrilled for him. And I was so very sad for myself. Ray had been the best boss I could have ever imagined. I tried to fill the emptiness I felt by telling him I was happy for him. He had earned it. Tucson will be a great place to retire.

He told me about his replacement. I was only half listening. It's like your dad saying, "I'm going to die in the next month. But let me tell you about your new dad, the one I helped your mother pick out..." I didn't want to hear about whoever was coming next. There could be no replacement for Ray.

Since this information was not to be made public for a few more days, I could not say anything, even to my management team. I had a choice to make. I could let everyone know that I was struggling. I could show my misery on my face. I could start to disengage and pull away while I tried to process what this information meant to me. Or I could choose to be happy.

Whenever I'd come home, Bruno would make me feel good. I couldn't help but get a boost when I'd see his shining face and little stump of a tail wagging! Bruno made me want to make other people feel that way.

Bruno may have been a secondhand dog, but he had an A-1 attitude.

I chose to be happy at this retreat, despite the news about my boss leaving. I threw myself into the activities, the work, and the fun. I even sang a little karaoke. Some of those people in the room would never have the opportunity to know Ray as I had known him. I wanted to show them what it was like to work for someone as classy as Ray had been to me. The retreat was a success. Just as the news was released by a corporate memo, I was telling my team what was happening and what to expect. They heard it from me, and I was able to answer their questions.

I had managed, coordinated, and attended many, many planning retreats during the time I had been in that company. Some of them were bare bones; some of them were galas. Because of the choice I had made to be happy and make this a memorable event for those around me, it ended up being one of the best meetings I've been part of.

What do people see when they see your face? Every facial expression, gesture, and ounce of body language is read by all observers.

What's on your face? If you are a leader, be sensitive to the messages you are sending. Employees can get fearful, distracted and insecure during tough times, and they look for signs in everything they see. What does your expression say to your employees? Do they see fear, frustration, or exhaustion? Or do they see confidence, hope, and optimism?

Does your family think that you are happy? This is important. A few years ago, my son would beg me to quit my job. He argued that I was gone all of the time, and when I was home, I was too tired to do anything fun. Yes, that's the kid perspective. But you know what? He was right that I had given my all at work, and I was very tired when I got home. My son thought I would be happier if I worked somewhere locally so I could be home more often for him. What I learned from him was that I needed to show him that I loved my job...and that I loved him. Sometimes duties conflict, but it was my job to make the most of both situations, and show that I took both roles seriously. I couldn't be home with my kids every day all day while providing for them. (Of course, I blame my non-trust-fund parents for their lack of financial planning).

Struggling with feeling happy on the inside? Try to bring a little joy to someone else. That good feeling you get from giving will make happiness move inside of you. Bruno chose to be happy, and he made me happy.

We all have our own happiness busters: those regular, inevitable events that elevate our blood pressure and lower our happiness. What is yours? It might be a long line in the store when you are in a hurry. Perhaps it's the inconsiderate driver who cuts in front of you. Maybe it's the neighbors' dog relieving himself on your lawn.

 1. Write down a few of the events in your life that get you upset, that bust your happiness.

2. Then, write how you typically respond to these events.

3. Finally, fill in the **TELL YOURSELF THIS** section to create self-talk that will counter the disappointments as they creep into your day.

HAPPINESS BUSTER	TYPICAL RESPONSE	TELL YOURSELF THIS

The key is not to fix or remove the happiness busters in our lives. Rather, it is to anticipate them and practice our responses to them in advance. I was counseling someone not long ago around impulse control. The boy said: I'm usually really good, but I get upset when I don't get my way. I can hear my mom saying, "It's easy to be an angel when no one ruffles your wings." I suggested that the boy anticipate that he will, indeed, not get his own way. Plan on that happening. Go into each situation expecting to be disappointed. Then, if he ends up getting his own way, he is pleasantly surprised instead of bitterly disappointed.

Bruno never read a self-help book or never attended a workshop on finding happiness. Bruno's Law could be summed up like this:

Things that make my tail wag make me happy. And things that make other tails wag make me happy, too.

Finally friends.

Lesson 8: Pay it forward.

It was a Sunday during tax season. Bruno and I had spent the morning wrapped under an afghan in our overstuffed papasan chair. We read, cuddled, and moved as little as possible. It was a nice morning. We were making the most of our time because the afternoon was going to be spent doing taxes. Yuck.

While we "adults" poured over W-2s, WD-40s, or whatever, Bruno was given a new rawhide chew toy to keep him occupied. Next to squeaky toys or stuffed animals, Bruno loved rawhide. This rawhide was enormous, as long as Bruno's body and probably half his weight. He plopped down next to the coffee table where we were working and set into gnawing on a corner of his new friend.

My wife and I jumped into mounds of paperwork. Unless you're a tax accountant, this stuff is impossible to figure out. We decided to take a break from work and get something to drink. We returned to the coffee table and plopped down on the couch.

While we talked, Bruno must have gotten a little lonely there on the floor so he picked up his new toy and looked up at the couch where the "adults" were sitting. He reared back and launched himself up. But the weight of the rawhide pulled him down. Instead of clearing the couch, his front legs and paws made it to the top but the rest of him couldn't make it up. He fell backwards with the rawhide still in his mouth, and his head hit the coffee table with a sickening thud.

He let out one cry. And he was gone. His neck was broken, and so was I.

From the day I brought him home, I dreaded this moment. I knew it was inevitable, but I thought it would be much further down the road. Not here, not now. Not because of a stupid toy, a secondhand coffee table, a desire to sit with us. Very selfishly, I hoped it would take place when I was far from home. I could never bring myself to imagine this taking place in my living room while I watched, his little fragile body growing cold in my hands, knowing with finality that I would never again hear his high-pitched bark, feel his wet nose against my toes at night, sense his intense gaze demanding that I throw his ball, or see his face light up when I returned home.

It would be years before I could bring myself to remember the details of that day, years longer before I could write about it. Bruno was my first dog. He was supposed to have been a beautiful little puppy and not the hunchbacked, high-strung defect that I brought home. He was supposed to reach at least 120 in dog years. He was supposed to be the grand, old, wise dog that watched over my children when they were born.

This was a defining event. I should have embraced that life was a great gift, and I should have taken great satisfaction that Bruno went out exactly like he lived: fast, passionate, and true to himself. He was doing what he loved to do, and he was in the company of those he loved.

But right that minute, I wasn't ready for the lessons. For a while, I went in the other direction. I grew bitter, and I pulled away.

There were to be other animals in my life. Milo, I mentioned. Additionally, there were Gino and Velvet (obviously, I didn't name that last one). None of these suffered accidental deaths. But all of them got old. The time came one by one when the veterinarian advised that it was time to say goodbye. Milo, Bruno's child-bride, was the first. I said goodbye to her, and then I scheduled to be out of town on the day of her passing. My wife emailed me on my cell phone to say that it was over. Milo was no more. I was sitting alone in a dark Texas bar trying to hide the tears that kept falling.

Velvet was next. Again, I took to the road right before he was going to pass.

Gino was my last Yorkie. He was very dear to me in his own right, but he was extra special because I believed Bruno's spirit had been reborn in him. He had the same passion and zeal for life that his "grandfather" had had. By the time Gino was nearing the end, he was a shadow of his former self. His eyesight and hearing were gone, arthritis prevented him from standing, and he couldn't control his bodily functions. It was time.

When I said goodbye to my little friend, I flashed back to saying goodbye to Bruno twenty years earlier. Gino was lying on the couch surrounded by pillows, and his head rested on a little stuffed animal. When I put my hand in front of him, he opened his mouth and gently bit my fingers. This was the only way he could identify people. Knowing it was me, he licked my hand and tried to get up.

I cried throughout the night. This time I determined to go to the veterinarian with my wife the next day.

While the "adults" drove to the vet, we retold stories about our special little boy, starting with the day we got him. Gino sat on my lap and soaked up my tears. While we waited for the doctor, Gino wagged his little tail and licked my hand. My hand was still wet when the doctor said, "He's gone."

Ray left at a great time. Or, I should say, he got out just in time. The nation's economy was sinking into a deep recession. We worked in the healthcare industry, an industry that was the topic of conversation by leading presidential candidates from both parties. After the presidential election, healthcare organizations were as popular as a cold sore. Customers were leaving our company, further straining profitability. The new executive vice president of internal operations was hired for her knowledge of the industry, but her real selling point was her experience in cutting cost.

I flashed back to a conversation I'd had with Ray when he asked me to take the position as his chief of staff.

"The chief of staff position reports to me, not just whoever is in the executive vice president role at the moment. The next EVP will likely bring in his or her own chief of staff, someone he or she has worked well with previously. Can you live with that, knowing that when I leave, you will need to find something else?"

I knew when I accepted my position that I had an expiration date. Once Ray left, I would become a secondhand chief of staff. Could I live with that? Absolutely. The opportunity to learn from the man who was a wonderful mentor was not something I could pass up.

I met with my new boss shortly after she joined the organization. She was nice enough. We talked in her office for twenty minutes. She asked a lot of questions and gave me quite a few assignments. She never offered me a chair. I think Jerry Seinfeld would have called her a *stand-talker*.

I knew that I wouldn't be there much longer.

I introduced her to the division by conducting and publishing an interview with her, and creating a presentation for her to take on the road so she could gain exposure to the eighty percent of the company that she had inherited. She conducted a keynote speech and a getting-to-know-you presentation that I prepared for her to deliver to all managers and officers in her division. I scheduled other meetings for her with employee groups across the organization so she could outline the business challenges and her vision for the company. Her message was a tough one: The economy is struggling, customers are leaving our company, and we need to lower cost to compete. Our biggest cost is employees. Guess what that means?

I wanted to make sure that my own team had as much information as I could provide. Our team owned and managed the typical internal mass-media outlets, so it was challenging to provide them with information they didn't already know. Instead of letting them hear things for the first time from our new boss in these formal meetings, I shared as much information as I could with them that was based on my personal observations and experiences with her.

Inevitably, during a team meeting, a question was directed to me from an employee who I knew I could count on to cut through the newspeak: Are our jobs on the line? Should we be worried?

There was tension in the room. Outside, overlooking Lake Michigan, we could all see the economy sinking on cement shoes. There was a cloud of healthcare-reform blood in the water. Customers could be seen from other office windows clipping $0.50-off coupons, valid for switching to our competition.

What would I want my boss to say to me in this situation? How had my boss prepared me for the inevitability of change? What would Bruno do?

Bruno may have been a secondhand dog, but he was a top-notch teacher.

While Bruno didn't live long enough for me to show him that I had learned everything he modeled for me, I did eventually learn. I learned that sometimes concentration must mean shutting out everything that doesn't take me closer to my goal. I learned that I can't do everything on my own; I need to put aside pride and ask for help. I learned to really listen and not just fake it. I learned to stand up for the things that matter. I learned to stifle fear enough to go outside of my comfort zone. I learned that I require much forgiveness so I cannot be stingy in the forgiveness that I offer others. I learned to find the good and to hold onto it even when everything else turns ugly.

It was time to pay it forward.

I answered, "I don't know how to answer that question, but I would guess that all noncore operation areas are on the table." My area was noncore. We did not deal directly with external, paying customers. Looking around the room, I saw fear.

"This might not help you, but let me tell you how I'm choosing to view my own job security." I took a deep breath. I was going to be honest and vulnerable. And I also wanted to be helpful. "If I were in the wilderness, a place surrounded with dangerous, wild animals, I wouldn't want coffee to keep me alert. I wouldn't want a rifle with a scope so I could see what was coming at me and protect myself. What I would most want is a good book." I looked up at a sea of blank faces, a couple of them wearing a slight, sad expression of sympathy that read, *he's lost it.*

I continued. "Why would I want to be hyper-aware and even more scared to death than normal during my last few hours to live? I'd rather be focused on the work in front of me, doing what I love to do, like being lost inside a good book. People shifted in their chairs. They were listening.

"So here's the way I'm choosing to look at things. I can be so concerned about my own job security that I'm paralyzed with fear: too afraid to make decisions, lead, or be productive. Or I can choose to act differently. If I'm to go out, I want it to happen while I'm concentrating on my tasks and working hard, instead of while I'm looking around anticipating all of the scary things that could pounce on me from the dark forest. I don't want to spend my last hours worrying. *Worrying won't change the outcome. But worrying will change me. And that's not how I want to be remembered."* This time there were several nods from my team.

My job, along with hundreds of others, was eliminated the following week.

I don't know about the others, but I am proud to say that I went out like Bruno: fast, passionate, and true to myself. I've learned to get up and move on, to create something beyond loss. I've learned to give even when the world doesn't give back. I've learned to live each day fully, giving to each experience wholeheartedly, accepting change and loss gracefully. I've learned that today is fleeting, and I won't consider any moment a waste if I am doing what I love and am with the ones I love. I've learned that life has no checklist, and I don't plan to wake up some day and say "I'm done! I finished everything on my list."

I've learned to live in the moment while looking forward to tomorrow, like Bruno did. And I'm still learning new things every day.

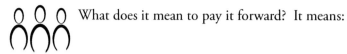 What does it mean to pay it forward? It means:

🐾 Taking the lessons you've learned and sharing them with others;
🐾 Treating people the way you want them to treat you; or, even better, treating people the way they most want to be treated; and
🐾 Turning each experience into a way to help others.

I was walking in a local cemetery the other day, and I saw that two women on opposite sides of the graveyard had passed away on the same day. In addition to sharing a common death date, both markers said, "Loving Mother." I wondered if these two women had similar parenting styles, similar personalities, or took a similar approach to life. That they loved their children and wanted the best things for them is what most parents can say. However, the specific lessons or the legacy that these two women left may have been very different.

Review the first exercise in the book. Look at the various **ROLES** you play at different times of your day and life. Look at the **KEY WORDS**, and then look at the **BEHAVIORS THAT SHOW IT**. It is very likely that you will be remembered. How intentional are you about creating that legacy now with every act you do?

1. Given the limited space on a grave marker, you are restricted to a few chosen words. Pretend you are writing your grave inscription now. What words do you want to be uttered by each of the **GROUPS/INDIVIDUALS** that apply?

GROUPS/INDIVIDUALS	INSCRIPTION
Family	
Spouse/Significant Other	
Children	
Grandchildren	
Parents	
Work	
Colleagues	
Boss	
Employees	
Customers	
Others	
God	
Neighbors	
Friends	
Acquaintances	
Strangers	

2. As long as we have the capability to learn and the capacity to teach others, our work improving our world is never complete. Put a star next to any of the **GROUPS/INDIVIDUALS** above that you want to give back to or that you want to make your priority.

We are the result of many who **PAID IT FORWARD** to us. These are individuals who taught us some important life lessons. I have a long list of those who role-modeled for me, believed in me, taught me, mentored me, gave me a chance...and sometimes even gave this secondhand dog a second chance:

- My parents who probably thought at times that reform school or prison were in my future, thank you.
- Every school teacher who ever pushed me, challenged me, refused to let me coast, thank you.
- My children who practice patience and show love to their old dad, thank you.
- Ray who saw something in me and gave me a chance to learn and grow at work, thank you.
- My former co-workers and employees who shared some incredible experiences with me, thank you.
- My friends who not only bring me laughter and joy but also dare me to be my best, thank you.

3. Make a list of those who have **PAID IT FORWARD** to you. Tell them. Thank them. Make sure they know that you noticed and appreciate the kindness they showed in you.

WHO?	TAUGHT ME WHAT?

4. Take it to the next level. Take the lessons that you've learned along your journey, and share them with others. And remember that no experience in our life is regrettable if we learned from it; this is even more true if we help others learn from it, too.

Saying Goodbye.

Prologue.

Pets have the ability to change the behaviors of their owners much more significantly than owners can change the behaviors of their pets. How many times have you had a wake-up bark early in the morning because your little canine friend thought it might be a lovely time to go for a walk? Or how many times has your furry feline pounced on you at three a.m. for no other reason than because **I'm a cat and I can?**

If we are tuned in, our pets can do more than change our routines and behaviors; they can change the way we think and live. Years ago, I had a little, four-pound dog named Bruno. My first impression of this little secondhand dog was not good. He was mean, yippy, and unkempt. After a short period, I came to understand that he was just being a little defensive because life had not been fair to him.

Years ago, a good friend passed a quote on to me from John Harrigan: "People need loving most when they deserve it the least." That's also true of animals. If I based my ability and desire to love Bruno based on my first impression, he would have never made his way into the backseat of my car or the forefront of my heart.

Bruno ended up teaching me many things, more than just not to leave a plate of pasta unattended on the table. He taught me how to get more out of life, how to treat other people, and how to be good with myself. I have tried to live my life mindful of the lessons Bruno taught me. Granted, I don't drink out of the toilet or skid my butt against the carpet like he did. But I try to practice his good character traits whenever I can.

Years after Bruno passed, I moved away from the Upper Peninsula of Michigan where I had been a family therapist. I moved back to the Chicago area to take a new job. I was hired as a management development specialist in the human resources department for the largest non investor-owned health insurance company in the nation. On my first day, I brought a few things to the office so the place would feel less sterile. The first item I unpacked was an 8 by 10 inch picture of Bruno lying half buried in our papasan chair. I had taken the picture a few hours before he died.

A coworker, Michelle, commented on the picture, "Your dog is so cute!"

"He was my little boy," I said. "He's gone now. But I learned a lot from him."

Maybe I'll have the opportunity to do that in this job, I thought to myself.

Michelle, it turned out, was a dog owner and lover. So I opened up a little more, "Let me tell you about this little guy named Bruno. Bruno may have been a secondhand dog, but he was my first-rate friend..."

This is my story about how two secondhand dogs helped each other have the best life imaginable.

96

Written by Scott Carbonara
Cover design by Chris Popieluszko